180093

**92
MON**

Rothaus, James R.   13031

Joe Montana

#381
Memphis City School
Title VI 99/808

**CHRIST METHODIST DAY SCHOOL
LIBRARY**

Joe Montana

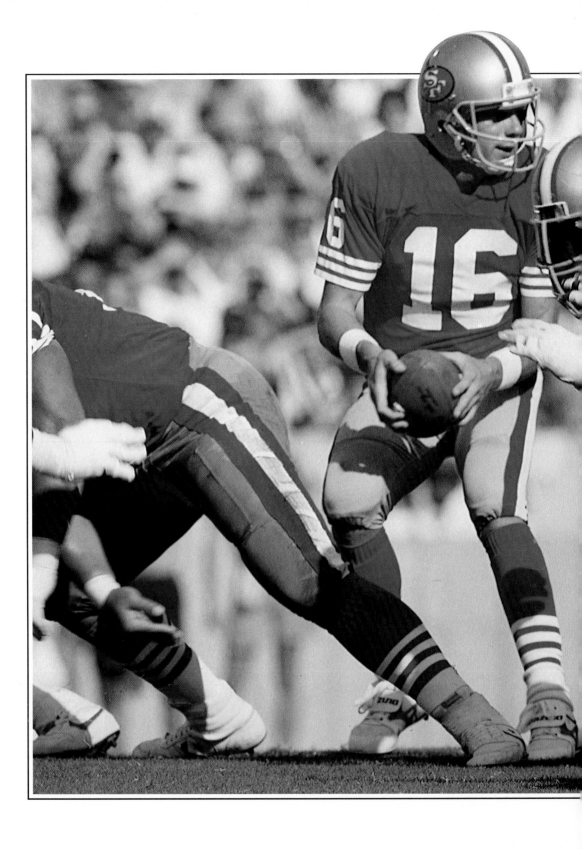

PHOTO CREDITS
All Photos by Michael Zagaris

Distributed to Schools and Libraries
in the United States by
ENCYCLOPAEDIA BRITANNICA EDUCATIONAL CORP.

310 S. Michigan Avenue
Chicago, Illinois 60604

Library of Congress Cataloging-in-Publication Data
Rothaus, James.
Joe Montana / Jim Rothaus.
p. cm.
Summary: Examines the life and career of the San Francisco 49ers
quarterback who is the highest rated passer in the history of the
National Football League.
ISBN 0-89565-736-8
1. Montana, Joe, 1956-   —Juvenile literature.
2. Football players–United States–Biography–Juvenile literature.
3. Quarterback (Football)–United States–Biography–Juvenile literature.
[1. Montana, Joe, 1956-   2. Football players.] I. Title.
GV939.M59R68 1991   91-17334
796.332′092–dc20   CIP
[B]   AC

Joe Montana

by James R. Rothaus

Montana takes the field.

It didn't look good for the San Francisco 49ers. They were behind the Cincinnati Bengals 16-13 with three minutes left in the 1989 Super Bowl. The 49ers had the ball on their eight yard line. If San Francisco was going to win its third Super Bowl title in seven years, the team would have to score on this drive. There would be no other chances.

As 49er quarterback Joe Montana stood on the sideline, he knew his teammates were nervous. Montana decided to do a little joking around. He walked over to tackle Harris Barton and said, "Hey, check it out." Barton didn't know what Montana was talking about. "Check what out?" Barton said to Montana. The quarterback pointed to the stands and said, "There's [actor] John Candy." Barton then grabbed a couple of teammates and told them to look for John Candy.

Montana goes over a play.

10

"**T**hen I got hold of myself," Barton recalled. "What was I doing?" He was doing exactly what Montana had hoped. Barton now was more relaxed, and so were several members of the 49er offense. "Fifteen seconds later," Barton said, "we're in the huddle. Joe's clapping his hands and saying, 'Hey, you guys want it? Let's go.'" The 49ers did go, all the way down the field. Led by a confident, calm quarterback, San Francisco marched ninety-two yards.

11

T he winning touchdown was a ten-yard pass from Montana to wide receiver John Taylor that gave the 49ers a 20-16 victory. The score came with thirty-four seconds left in the game. On the Cincinnati sideline, Bengal coach Sam Wyche stared at the ground. He couldn't believe what Montana had done. "Thirty-four seconds," Wyche said to himself. "We were thirty-four seconds from winning the game." But Wyche knew that no lead was ever safe when Joe Montana was leading the other team.

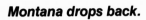

Joe calls out the signals.

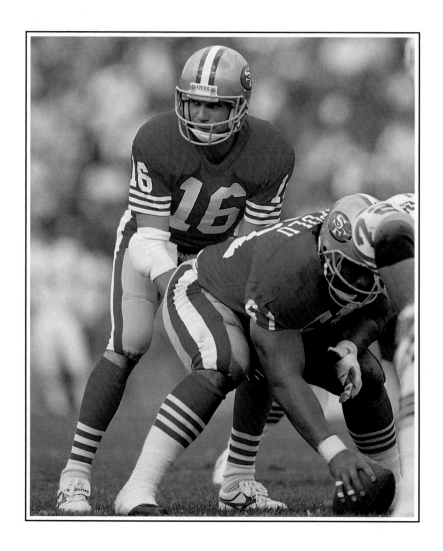

14

Wyche had been an assistant coach for the 49ers in the early 1980s. That was when a young Joe Montana led the team to the top of the National Football League. Wyche had watched as Montana grew into one of the best quarterbacks in the NFL. Montana also became known as a master of the comeback victory. But that was nothing new to Joe. He had been leading his teams to amazing victories since he was eight years old.

15

Montana grew up in
Monongahela, Pennsylvania. As an
eight-year-old, he played for a team
called the Little Wildcats. It played
in a peewee league in Joe's home-
town. Montana's first coach was Carl
Crawley. Crawley saw right away
that Montana was a born leader.
"He wanted to win, and he'd do
whatever it took," Crawley remem-
bered. "That's another thing the
kids liked about him. With Joe on
the field, they knew they were never
out of any game."

Ten years later Montana was playing college football at the University of Notre Dame. He was still known as a leader and a winner. "Whenever he came on the field, the players knew they had a friend coming in," said Bob Golic, one of Montana's teammates at Notre Dame. Montana's first amazing comeback at Notre Dame came in 1975. The Fighting Irish were behind North Carolina 14-6 with five minutes left in the game. Montana didn't start the game, but he came off the bench and led Notre Dame to a 21-14 win.

After the game Notre Dame athletic director Moose Krause ran up to Irish coach Dan Devine and shook his hand. "Fantastic," Krause said. "Greatest comeback I've ever seen." One week later Montana came off the bench with the Irish trailing Air Force 30-10 in the fourth quarter. He threw two touchdown passes as the Irish pulled out a 31-30 victory. "In the locker room after the game, Moose said, 'This one's better than last week,'" Devine recalled.

But Montana saved his best performance at Notre Dame for his last college game. In the 1979 Cotton Bowl against Houston, the Irish fell behind 34-12 in the fourth quarter. The game was played during an ice storm. Some players got sick, including Montana. He spent most of the second half in the locker room. His body temperature had dropped to 96 degrees. Notre Dame's trainers tried everything to raise Montana's temperature. They even fed him chicken soup.

It must have worked, because Montana returned to the field with eight minutes left. He threw two touchdown passes as the Irish won 35-34. The winning score came on the last play of the game. It was a six-yard pass from Montana to wide receiver Kris Haines in the corner of the end zone. "Joe threw a perfect pass," Devine said. "He was so calm. I swear he was no different than he would have been in practice." Montana then was drafted by the San Francisco 49ers.

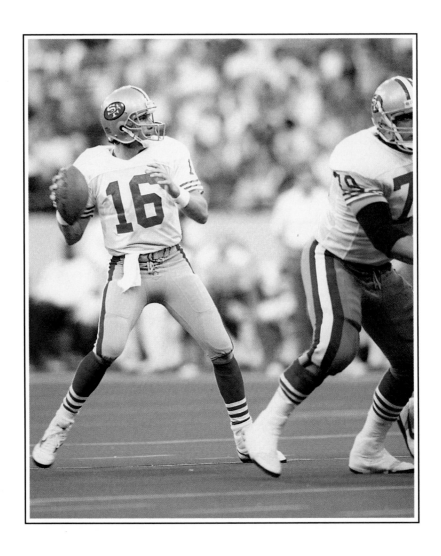

San Francisco Makes the Playoffs

The young quarterback soon showed he still had the ability to lead amazing comebacks. In only his third season in pro ball, Montana led the 49ers to the 1981 NFL playoffs. San Francisco won its first playoff game. That moved the 49ers into the game for the conference championship against the Dallas Cowboys. Dallas led 27-21 with four minutes left. Then Montana took over. He drove the 49ers ninety-one yards. Montana hit Dwight Clark with the winning touchdown pass.

San Francisco went on to beat the Cincinnati Bengals in the Super Bowl that year 26-21. Joe Montana was named the game's most valuable player. Three years later Montana and the 49ers won another Super Bowl. They beat Miami 38-16. Montana again was given the MVP award. In 1989 and 1990, the 49ers also won Super Bowl titles. The 1990 team finished the season with a 55-10 Super Bowl victory over Denver. Montana had one of his finest games as a pro. He threw five touchdown passes to set a Super Bowl record. He was named MVP of the Super Bowl for the third time.

After Montana's performance against Denver, some experts began calling him the greatest quarterback ever. And why not. He is the highest rated passer in NFL history. But Montana's most amazing statistic is that he has led twenty-three fourth-quarter comeback victories in the NFL. Of course, Joe has been working miracles on the football field since he was eight years old. Why should he stop now?